The Greatest Gift

A Christmas Puppet Play

Puppets for JESUS!

Winning the lost, strengthening faith
& equipping the saints through
the power of God's word.
PuppetsForJESUS.com

Copyright © Puppets for JESUS!

PuppetsForJESUS.com All rights reserved.

The contents in this book may be copied and reproduced for the use of performing the puppet play contained within for non-profit Christian ministry only. No further permission is required to use the contents contained within for non-profit Christian ministry. The materials in this book may only be used as listed above and may not be used in any effort to contradict any portion of the contents of this publication. No portion of this publication may be published, transmitted, reproduced, or distributed in any form including but not limited to internet, electrical, mechanical, photocopying, recording, or any other form without prior written consent from the author.

Contents

Performing Options 4

Meet The Characters 5

The Greatest Gift 6

Object Lesson 20

Thinkers 22

Performing Options

Navigating between the performance options is simple. You can choose to include audience participation and add music to your performance or you can choose to omit the music and perform the puppet play all the way through.

♫ ♪♩ ♬ ♭ MUSIC: If you choose to include music in your performance then you will simply continue the skit into the area that is defined as *Praise Break*. Each *Praise Break* is clearly defined and includes three song suggestions that you can sing with your audience. You can choose to sing one or more songs based on your needs. You can also choose to sing different songs. The songs you choose are totally up to you. It's a great way to get your audience up on their feet and participating in the action.

SKIT ONLY: If you would rather skip over the singing and only perform the puppet play, simply ignore the lines that are inside of the *Praise Break* area. Your puppet play will flow seamlessly either way.

Meet The Characters

Katie is cute, sassy and bubbling with excitement for Christmas. Well, it's the Christmas presents that has so her excited, not the true meaning of Christmas. She knows that Christmas is about celebrating the birth of Jesus and his great love for us, but she got more focused on the gifts she would be getting instead of Jesus, the best gift of all.

Zeek is a young genius who is into building robots, computers and making the world a better place with his inventions. The only thing Zeek loves more than tinkering with electronics is telling others about Jesus. He helps Katie get back on tack and together they tell the true story of The Greatest Gift.

> Every good and perfect gift is from above, coming down from the Father of the heavenly lights, who does not change like shifting shadows.
> James 1:17

The Greatest Gift
A Christmas Puppet Play

Katie: *(enters singing in the tune of Santa Claus is Coming to Town)* I'm making a list and checking it twice… I want a lot of things and getting stuff's nice. My presents are coming to town… My presents are coming to town… My presents are coming to town!

Zeek: Whoa! Let's recalculate this! Your presents are coming to town? You act as if it's YOUR birthday.

Katie: It's better than a birthday; it's presents day!

Zeek: Unfortunately, that is what so many people think in the *present* day.

Katie: The present day! You got it, my main geek! The day of the gifts!

Zeek: Not present day as in gift day but present day as in the present, the here and now, today is the present and not the past.

Katie: You act like getting presents is a bad thing.

Zeek: Not at all. I like getting gifts, but some people act like that's what Christmas is all about.

Katie: Isn't Christmas all about gifts?

Zeek: Well... Christmas is about the greatest gift of all.

Katie: The Super Transforming Diva Pet Shop Beauty Queen Poodle Pooch Parlor? That is the greatest gift of em all!

Zeek: No! The super transinkle diva do pretty pooch parlor whats-a-ma-hinkle is NOT the greatest gift of all!

Katie: It's The Super Transforming Diva Pet Shop Beauty Queen Poodle Pooch Parlor!

Zeek: Whatever... It is not the greatest gift.

Katie: Do they already have version 323.0 out? Every time I think I got the latest version they make a new one and I have to buy another. I wonder if they do that on purpose.

Zeek: Ya think? The point is, the greatest gift of all is not a what, but a who.

Katie: A who?

Zeek: Yes, Jesus Christ is the greatest gift of all. We celebrate Christmas because it is Jesus' birthday, not ours.

Katie: That's right, Zeek! It is Jesus' birthday. I get so excited about getting presents that I forget what Christmas is all about. After all, Christmas does begin with Christ. I know Christmas is all about Jesus, but why do we call Jesus the greatest gift of all?

Zeek: Jesus is the Son of God who left his home in heaven to be born as a human person. He was fully God and became fully man.

Katie: I know the story. A young couple named Mary and Joseph were engaged to be married when an angel came to Mary and told her that she would give birth to God's son, and he would be the savior of the entire world! However, these things confused and upset Joseph, he wasn't sure what to believe, but an angel came to Joseph and told him that the baby Mary was carrying was God's only son. Can you image? So, Mary and Joseph were married, and they loved each other very much. They had the best baby shower in the world! The birth announcements were the grandest ever! Jesus had all the best gifts!

♫♪♩♫♭ Praise Break ♭♫♩♪♫

Zeek: It's completely epic! An angel from God told Mary that she would have a son, his name would be Jesus, and he would be the savior of the entire world!

Katie: It makes me want to sing!

Zeek: That's something that we can agree on!

Katie: Come on, everyone, stand up and sing with us! *(music begins to play as puppets exit)*

♫♪♩♫♭ Joy to the World
♫♪♩♫♭ Mary Did You Know
♫♪♩♫♭ Gabriel's Message

Zeek: I'm so glad you're finally starting to focus on the real meaning of Christmas.

Katie: Me too! Now back to the fancy story about the best baby shower in the world, the grandest birth announcements and the fancy gifts. I know it's not all about the gifts, but I do love the fancy part.

♫♪♩♫♭ End Praise Break ♭♫♩♪♫

Zeek: What? I thought you said you knew the story.

Katie: Didn't I tell it right?

Zeek: Up until the part about Jesus having the best baby shower in the world, the grandest birth announcements ever and all the best gifts! You must not have listened to the WHOLE story in Sunday school.

Katie: I bet ya I did. I know a grand entrance when I see one.

Zeek: I'll tell this true story, and you'll see that Jesus entered the world without any of the things that you've said.

Katie: If I'm right, you'll have to drink my eggnog!

Zeek: Your recipe stinks to high heaven! Last time I drank it… well… let's just say you know what happened to my cookies.

Katie: I still think it was the cookies that made you toss my eggnog!

Zeek: It was your eggnog that made me toss my cookies!

Katie: Okay, but you're going to be drinking it again and you'll see that it tastes as good as the way I told the story is true.

Zeek: Not going to happen because Jesus was born in a barn. Mary and Joseph had to travel seventy miles to Bethlehem because the king ordered everyone to travel back to the city of their birth to be counted.

Katie: They didn't have cars back then. Mary had to ride on a donkey and Joseph walked all that way and to top it off, when they arrived in Bethlehem, they couldn't find a room to rent, and they had nowhere to sleep.

Zeek: But Mary and Joseph didn't complain. A nice man let them stay in his barn and they were thankful. Mary gave birth to Jesus, and they wrapped him in swaddling clothes and laid him in a manger. It was a very humble entrance for the great King, indeed.

♫♪♩♬♭ Praise Break ♭♫♩♪♫

Katie: I can't believe that Jesus was born in a barn. The Savior of the world didn't even have a bed, they laid him in a manger. Hey, what even is a manger?

Zeek: A manger is a trough that animals eat or dink out of. See? There isn't any fancy parts in this story so I won't be drinking any of your puke-nog. Sorry, I mean eggnog.

Katie: Zeek! You'll be drinking it because the story does get fancy, you just wait and see, but thinking about Jesus being born in a manger reminds me of a song. Will you sing it with me?

Zeek: Sure, we all will. Everyone stand to your feet and join us. *(music begins to play as puppets exit)*

♫♪♩♬♭ Silent Night
♫♪♩♬♭ Away in a Manger
♫♪♩♬♭ O Little Town of Bethlehem

♫♪♩♬♭ End Praise Break ♭♫♩♪♫

Katie: Now for the fancy part! I just love the fancy part! You stop me if I get anything wrong. Get ready for my famous eggnog surprise!

Zeek: The fancy part? What fancy part? I'll be stopping you because there isn't any fancy part.

Katie: When Jesus was born, off in a field in the same country, shepherds were watching and tending their sheep. An angel appeared before the shepherds and God's glory shined all around them. The shepherds were so afraid. It's not every day somebody comes before you glowing!

Zeek: I would really be afraid nowadays if somebody was glowing. Too much nuclear waste! Go green!

Katie: Zeek! You really are a geek! But I agree, recycle!

Zeek: Thank you! I think...

Katie: Anyhow... The angel told the shepherds...

Zeek: *"Fear not: for, behold, I bring you good tidings of great joy, which shall be to all people. For unto you is born this day in the city of David a Savior, which is Christ the Lord. And this shall be a sign unto you; Ye shall find the babe wrapped in swaddling clothes, lying in a manger."*

Katie: *"And suddenly there was with the angel a multitude of the heavenly host praising God, and saying, Glory to God in the highest, and on earth peace, good will toward men."* *(music begins to play as puppets exit)*

♫ ♪♩ ♫ ♭ Praise Break ♭ ♫ ♩ ♪ ♫

Katie: Angels singing and praising God must've been the most beautiful sound the world has ever heard.

Zeek: Do you know what sounds even more beautiful to God?

Katie: More beautiful than angels singing? What could sound more beautiful to God than angels praising him?

Zeek: God's people praising and singing to him is the most beautiful sound unto God's ears, even more beautiful than angels.

Katie: Let's sing a song to God together. Stand up and sing it loud! *(music begins to play as puppets exit)*

♫ ♪♩ ♫ ♭ Hark! The Herald Angels Sing
♫ ♪♩ ♫ ♭ Angels We Have Heard on High
♫ ♪♩ ♫ ♭ While Shepherds Watched Their Flocks

♫ ♪♩ ♫ ♭ End Praise Break ♭ ♫ ♩ ♪ ♫

Katie: WOW! The grandest birth announcement ever! Who else has had all of heaven open up to announce their birth? You better get ready for eggnog, Zeek!

Zeek: Okay, I'll give you that one. The birth announcement was pretty spectacular, but what about the baby shower and the gifts? I don't recall a baby shower.

Katie: *(sighs)* Oh, Zeek. What about the three wisemen? They saw the star of Bethlehem that God placed in the sky over the place where Jesus was born and King Herod asked them about the baby who he heard had been born King of the Jews.

Zeek: The wicked and foolish king thought Jesus would grow up and take over the kingdom, so he plotted to kill baby Jesus.

Katie: He told the three wisemen to find the baby and tell him where he was so he could go worship Jesus.

Zeek: Wisemen are called wise for a reason; they knew the king was lying and they left to go find Jesus with no intentions of ever returning and telling King Herod where Jesus was.

Katie: When they found Jesus, they showered him with gifts of gold, frankincense and myrrh. What a baby shower! Those were some pretty awesome gifts. You have to admit it!

Zeek: UGH! My stomach is turning already! You tricked me! Eggnog surprise, bluck!

Katie: I didn't mean to trick you, but you really did make me think about Jesus having all the best gifts.

Zeek: Gold, frankincense and myrrh? I am sure you like the part about getting expensive gifts.

Katie: When I say Jesus has the best gifts, I mean Jesus brings the best gifts into the world. He has all the best gifts and gives them to us. He gives us joy, peace and love.

Zeek: Through God's love and Jesus Christ, everyone can receive the best gift of all.

Katie: You're right, Zeek. There isn't any present better than the gift of salvation through Jesus Christ.

Zeek: Jesus is our gift from God who saves us from our sins.

Katie: When we believe that Jesus is God's only son born of a virgin and that he took the punishment for our sins by dying on the cross for us, and we ask him to come into our hearts and be Lord of our life, and we repent and ask for forgiveness of our sins then God wipes all our sins away. We are made new, and we receive God's gift of salvation.

Zeek: The best gift we can give to Jesus and others this Christmas is to simply tell them about God and his great love for them.

Katie: You can't unwrap a gift if you don't even know you have it.

Zeek: *(to the audience)* What kind of gift are you going to give this Christmas?

Katie: I'm going to give the best gift of all. I am going to tell everyone about Jesus and God's great love for them! You were right, Zeek, giving is better than receiving!

♫♪♩♬♭ Praise Break ♭♬♩♪♫

Katie: Jesus fills my heart with joy! I want to sing!

Zeek: We'll all join you.
(music begins to play as puppets exit)

♫♪♩♬♭ O Come, All Ye Faithful
♫♪♩♬♭ Go Tell It on the Mountain
♫♪♩♬♭ We Wish You a Merry Christmas

Katie: Thank you for reminding me about the real meaning of Christmas, Zeek. You're a good friend.

♫♪♩♬♭ End Praise Break ♭♬♩♪♫

Zeek: So, I don't have to drink the stink-nog, uh, I mean the eggnog?

Katie: Zeek Geek! Just for that you have to drink double! *(exit)*

Zeek: Wait! Come back here! I didn't mean it! *(exit)*

Object Lesson

YOU WILL NEED a big box (the bigger the better), Christmas wrapping paper and ribbons and bows to decorate the box. Something to place inside the box to represent salvation such as a cross, a nativity set or a giant heart to represent God's love.

Wrap the box in many layers with an abundance of wrapping paper and ribbons and bows. Call the children up one at a time and ask them how they can show somebody the love of Jesus. It's okay if answers are repeated. Allow each child to unwrap the gift a little bit at a time by removing one bow, ribbon or a portion of the paper. Explain that this is how it is when we tell others about Jesus.

When the gift is fully unwrapped, you can share what's inside.

Although it is up to everyone to choose for his or herself to accept Jesus and his wonderful gift of salvation, we can help others unwrap God's good gifts by telling them about Jesus and showing them God's love. After all, if they don't know about Jesus then how can they accept him and his good gifts?

How can we show others God's love? When we are kind, helpful and living for Jesus, it shows others God's good gifts at work inside of us.

 Thinkers

Bible Verse:

James 1:17 Every good and perfect gift is from above, coming down from the Father of the heavenly lights, who does not change like shifting shadows.

Every good gift comes from God!

Review Questions:

Who is the greatest gift of all? Jesus!

Why is Jesus the greatest gift to the world? Jesus is God's gift of love and salvation.

Whose birthday is it on Christmas?

What is the best gift we can give Jesus and others on Christmas? Tell them about Jesus.

What did Katie mean when she said, "You can't unwrap a gift if you don't even know that you have it?" For somebody to receive the gift of salvation, somebody else has to tell them about it.

How do we help others unwrap their gift of salvation? Tell them about Jesus and show them God's love with kindness.

Why do you think it is better to give than to receive?

What are some things you can do to spread the love of Jesus this season?

Every good and perfect gift is from above, coming down from the Father of the heavenly lights, who does not change like shifting shadows.
James 1:17

Puppets For JESUS!

Puppets For JESUS has been dedicated to winning the lost, strengthening faith and equipping the saints since 2000. To learn more about us and what we do, we invite you to visit us online at PuppetsForJESUS.com for puppet ministry resources and also at ChildrensChurchCurriculum.com for the most current and relevant children's and youth ministry curriculum. All our puppet skits, lesson plans, object lessons, sermons and curriculums are free for you to use in your ministry. Let's make heaven crowded!

…we will tell the next generation the praiseworthy deeds of the Lord, his power, and the wonders he has done.

Psalms 78:4

www.ingramcontent.com/pod-product-compliance
Lightning Source LLC
LaVergne TN
LVHW061326060426
835510LV00017B/1946